THE HISTORY OF THE PSYCHOANALYTIC MOVEMENT

BY

PROF. DR. SIGMUND FREUD, LL.D.

OF VIENNA

AUTHORIZED ENGLISH TRANSLATION BY

A. A. BRILL, Ph.B., M.D.

LECTURER IN PSYCHOANALYSIS AND ABNORMAL PSYCHOLOGY, NEW YORK UNIVERSITY
FORMER CHIEF OF CLINIC OF PSYCHIATRY, COLUMBIA UNIVERSITY

ISBN: 978-1-63182-953-6

Printed: March 2023

Published and Distributed By:
Lushena Books
607 Country Club Drive, Unit E
Bensenville, IL 60106
www.lushenabks.com

ISBN: 978-1-63182-953-6

NERVOUS AND MENTAL DISEASE MONOGRAPH SERIES

Edited by

Drs. SMITH ELY JELLIFFE and WM. A. WHITE

Numbers Issued

If in what follows I bring any contribution to the history of the psychoanalytic movement nobody must be surprised at the subjective nature of this paper, nor at the rôle which falls to me therein. For psychoanalysis is my creation; for ten years I was the only one occupied with it, and all the annoyance which this new subject caused among my contemporaries has been hurled upon my head in the form of criticism. Even today, when I am no longer the only psychoanalyst, I feel myself justified in assuming that none can know better than myself what psychoanalysis is, wherein it differs from other methods of investigating the psychic life, what its name should cover, or what might better be designated as something else.

In the year 1909, when I was first privileged to speak publicly on psychoanalysis in an American University, fired by this momentous occasion for my endeavors, I declared that it was not myself who brought psychoanalysis into existence. I said that it was Josef Breuer, who had merited this honor at a time when I was a student and busy working for my examinations (1880–1882).[1] Since then, well-intentioned friends have frequently repeated that I then expressed my gratitude out of all due proportion. They considered that, as on previous occasions, I should have dignified Breuer's "cathartic procedure" as merely preliminary to psychoanalysis, and should have claimed that psychoanalysis itself only began with my rejection of the hypnotic technique and my introduction of free association. Now it is really a matter of indifference whether the history of psychoanalysis be considered to have started with the cathartic method or only with my modification of

[1] "On Psychoanalysis." Five lectures given on the occasion of the twentieth anniversary of Clark University, Worcester, Mass., dedicated to Stanley Hall. Second edition, 1912. Published simultaneously in English in the American Journal of Psychology, March, 1910; translated into Dutch, Hungarian, Polish and Russian.

the same. I only enter into this uninteresting question because some opponents of psychoanalysis are wont to recall, now and then, that the art of psychoanalysis did not originate with me at all, but with Breuer. Naturally, this only happens to be the case when their attitude permits them to find in psychoanalysis something that is noteworthy; on the other hand when their repudiation of psychoanalysis is unlimited, then psychoanalysis is always indisputably my creation. I have never yet heard that Breuer's great part in psychoanalysis has brought him an equal measure of insult and reproach. As I have recognized long since that it is the inevitable fate of psychoanalysis to arouse opposition and to embitter people, I have come to the conclusion that I must surely be the originator of all that characterizes psychoanalysis. I add, with satisfaction, that none of the attempts to belittle my share in this much disdained psychoanalysis has ever come from Breuer himself, or could boast of his support.

The content of Breuer's discovery has been so often presented that a detailed discussion of it here may be omitted. Its fundamental fact is that the symptoms of hysterical patients depend upon impressive but forgotten scenes in their lives (traumata). The therapy founded thereon was to cause the patients to recall and reproduce these experiences under hypnosis (catharsis), and the fragmentary theory, deduced from it was that these symptoms corresponded to an abnormal use of undischarged sums of excitement (conversion). In his theoretical contribution to the "Studies of Hysteria" Breuer, wherever obliged to mention *conversion*, has always added my name in parenthesis, as though this first attempt at a theoretical formulation was my mental property. I think this allotment refers only to the nomenclature, whilst the conception itself occurred to us both at the same time.

It is also well known that Breuer, after his first experience with it, allowed the cathartic treatment to rest for a number of years and only resumed it after I caused him to do so, on my return from Charcot. He was then an internist and taken up with a rather busy medical practice. I had become a physician quite reluctantly but had, at that time, received a strong motive for desiring to help nervous patients or, at least, to learn to understand something of their conditions. I had placed reliance on physical therapy and found myself helpless in the face of disappointments that came to me with W. Erb's "Electrotherapy," so rich in advice and indications. If I did not, at that time, pilot myself independently to the opinion later announced by Moebius, that the successes of electrotherapy in nervous disorders are the results of suggestion, it was surely only the absence of these successes that was to blame. The treatment by *suggestion* in deep hypnosis seemed to offer me at that time sufficient compensation for the lost electrical therapy. I learned this treatment through the extremely impressive demonstrations of Liébault and Bernheim. But the investigation under hypnosis with which I became acquainted through Breuer, I found, owing to its automatic manner of working and the simultaneous gratification of one's eagerness for knowledge, much more attractive than the monotonous and violent suggestive command which was devoid of every possibility of inquiry.

As one of the latest achievements of psychoanalysis, we have lately been admonished to put the actual conflict and the cause of the illness into the foreground of analysis. This is exactly what Breuer and I did in the beginning of our work with the cathartic method. We guided the patient's attention directly to the traumatic scene during which the symptom had arisen, tried to find therein the psychic conflict and to free the repressed affect. We thus discovered the procedure characteristic of the psychic processes of the neuroses which I later named *regression*. The associations of the patients went back from the scene to be explained, to earlier experiences, and this forced the analysis which was to correct the present to occupy itself with the past. This regression led even further backwards. At first it went quite regularly to the time of puberty. Later, however, such failures as gaps in the understanding tempted the analytic work further back into the years of childhood which had, hitherto, been inaccessible to every sort of investigation. This regressive direction became an important characteristic of the analysis. / It was proved that psychoanalysis could not clear up anything actual, except by going back to something in the past. It even proved that every pathological experience presupposes an earlier one which, though not in itself pathological, lent a patho-' logical quality to the later occurrence. But the temptation to stop short at the known actual cause was so great that even in later analyses I yielded to it. In the case of the patient called "Dora," carried out in 1899, the scene which caused the outbreak of the actual illness was known to me. I tried uncounted times to analyse this experience, but all that I could receive to my direct demands was the same scanty and broken description. Only after a long detour, which led through the earliest childhood of the patient, a dream appeared in the analysis of which the hitherto forgotten details of the scene were remembered, and this made possible the understanding and solution of the actual conflict.

From this one example it may be seen how misleading is the above mentioned admonition and how much of a scientific regression it is to follow the advice of neglecting the regression in the analytic technique.

The first difference of opinion between Breuer and myself came to light on a question of the more intimate psychic mechanism of hysteria. He still favored a physiological theory, so to speak, and wished to explain the psychic splitting of consciousness of hysterical subjects by means of the non-communication of various psychic states (or states of consciousness, as we then called them). He thus created the theory of the "hypnoid states," the results of which were supposed to bring the unassimilated foreign body into the "waking consciousness." I had formulated this to myself less scientifically. I suspected everywhere tendencies and strivings analogous to those of everyday life and conceived the psychic split-ting itself as a result of a repelling process, which I then called "defense" and later "regression." I made a short-lived attempt to reconcile both mechanisms, but as experience showed me always the same and only one thing, my defense theory, I soon became opposed to Breuer's theory of hypnoid states.

I am, however, quite certain that this difference of opinion had nothing to do with the parting of the ways which occurred soon afterward between us. The latter had a deeper reason, but it happened in such a manner that at first I did not understand it, and only later did I learn to interpret it, following many good indexes. It will be recalled that Breuer had stated, concerning his first famous patient, that the sexual element had been astonishingly undeveloped in her and had never contributed anything to her very marked morbid picture.[2] I have always wondered why the critics of my theory of the sexual etiology of the neuroses have not often opposed it with this assertion of Breuer, and up to this day I do not know whether in this reticence I am to see a proof of their discretion, or of their lack of observation. Whoever will reread the history of Breuer's patient in the light of the experience gained in the last twenty years, will have no difficulty in understanding the symbolism of the snakes and of the arm. By taking into account also the situation at the sick-bed of the father, he will easily guess the actual meaning of that symptom-formation. His opinion as to the part sexuality played in the psychic life of that girl will then differ greatly from that of her physician. To cure the patient Breuer utilized the most intensive suggestive *rapport* which may serve us as prototype of that which we call "transference." Now I have strong grounds to suppose that Breuer, after the disposal of the symptoms, must have discovered the sexual motivity of this transference by new signs, but that the general nature of this unexpected phenomenon escaped him, so that here, as though hit by "an untoward event," he broke off the investigation. I did not obtain from him any direct information of this, but at different times he has given me sufficient connecting links to justify me in making this combination. And then, as I stood more and more decidedly for the significance of sexuality in the causation of the neuroses, Breuer was the first to show me those reactions of unwilling rejection, with which it was my lot to become so familiar later on, but which I had then not yet recognized as my unavoidable destiny.

[2] Breuer and Freud, "Studien über Hysterie," p. 15, Deuticke, 1895.

The fact that a grossly sexual, tender or inimical, transference occurs in every treatment of a neurosis, although this was neither desired nor induced by either party, has, for me, always seemed to be the most unshakable proof that the forces of the neuroses originate in the sexual life. This argument has surely not been seriously enough considered, for if it were, there would be no question as to where the investigation would tend. For my own conviction, it has remained decisive over and above the special results of the work of the analysis.

Some comfort for the bad reception which my theory of the sexual etiology of the neuroses met with, even in the closer circle of my friends—a negative space was soon formed about my person— I found in the thought that I had taken up the fight for a new and original idea. One day, however, my memories grouped themselves in such a way that this satisfaction was disturbed, but in return I obtained an excellent insight into the origin of our activities and into the nature of our knowledge. The idea for which I was held responsible had not at all originated with me. It had come to me from three persons, whose opinions could count upon my deepest respect; from Breuer himself, from Charcot, and from Chrobak, the gynecologist of our university, probably the most prominent of our Vienna physicians. All three men had imparted to me an insight which, strictly speaking, they had not themselves possessed. Two of them denied their communication to me when later I reminded them of this: the third (Master Charcot) might also have done so, had it been granted me to see him again. But these identical communications, received without my grasping them, had lain dormant within me, until one day they awoke as an apparently original discovery.

One day, while I was a young hospital doctor, I was accompanying Breuer on a walk through the town when a man came up to him urgently desiring to speak with him. I fell back and, when Breuer was free again, he told me, in his kindly, teacher-like manner, that this was the husband of a patient, who had brought him some news about her. The wife, he added, behaved in so conspicuous a manner when in company, that she had been turned over to him for treatment as a nervous case. He ended with the remark—"those are always secrets of the alcove." Astonished, I asked his meaning and he explained the expression to me ("secrets of the conjugal bed"), without realizing how preposterous the matter appeared to me.

A few years later, at one of Charcot's evening receptions, I found myself near the venerated teacher who was just relating to Brouardel a very interesting history from the day's practice. I did not hear the beginning clearly but gradually the story obtained my attention. It was the case of a young married couple from the far East. The wife was a great sufferer and the husband was impotent, or exceedingly awkward. I heard Charcot repeat: "Tâchez donc, je vous assure vous y arriverez." Brouardel, who spoke less distinctly, must have expressed his astonishment that symptoms as those of the young wife should have appeared as a result of such circumstances, for Charcot said suddenly and with great vivacity: "Mais, dans des cas pareils c'est toujours la chose génital, toujours—toujours—toujours." And while saying that he crossed his hands in his lap and jumped up and down several times, with the vivacity peculiar to him. I know that for a moment I was almost paralyzed with astonishment, and I said to myself: "Yes, but if he knows this why does he never say so?" But the impression was soon forgotten; brain-anatomy and the experimental production of hysterical paralysis absorbed all my interests.

A year later when I had begun my medical activities in Vienna as a private *dozent* in nervous diseases I was as innocent and ignorant in all that concerned the etiology of the neuroses as any promising academician could be expected to be. One day I received a friendly call from Chrobak, who asked me to take a patient to whom he could not give sufficient time in his new capacity as lecturer at the university. I reached the patient before he did and learned that she suffered from senseless attacks of anxiety, which could only be alleviated by the most exact information as to the whereabouts of her physician at any time in the day. When Chrobak appeared, he took me aside and disclosed to me that the patient's anxiety was due to the fact that though she had been married eighteen years, she was still a *virgo intacta*, that her husband was utterly impotent. In such cases the physician can only cover the domestic mishap with his reputation and must bear it if people shrug their shoulders and say of him: "He is not a good doctor if in all these years, he has not been able to cure her." He added: "The only prescription for such troubles is the one well-known to us, but which we cannot prescribe. It is:

Penis normalis

dosim

Repetatur!

I had never heard of such a prescription and would like to have shaken my head at my informant's cynicism.

I certainly have not uncovered the illustrious origins of this vicious idea because I would like to shove the responsibility for it on others. I know well that it is one thing to express an idea once or several times in the form of a rapid *aperçu,* and quite another to take it seriously and literally to lead it through all opposing details and conquer for it a place among accepted truths. It is the difference between a light flirtation and a righteous marriage with all its duties and difficulties. Epouser les idées de—(to marry so and so's ideas,) is, at least in French, a quite usual form of speech.

Other doctrines which were contributed to the cathartic method through my efforts thus transforming it into psychoanalysis, are the following: The theories of repression and resistance, the addition of the infantile sexuality, and the usage and interpretation of dreams for the understanding of the unconscious.

Concerning the theory of repression, I was certain that I worked independently. I knew of no influence that directed me in any way to it, and I long considered this idea to be original, till O. Rank showed us the place in Schopenhauer's "The World as Will and Idea," where the philosopher is struggling for an explanation for insanity.[3] What is there said concerning the striving against the acceptance of a painful piece of reality agrees so completely with the content of my theory of repression that, once again, I must be indebted to my not being well-read for the possibility of making a discovery. To be sure, others have read this passage and overlooked it, without making this discovery and perhaps the same would have happened to me, if, in former years, I had taken more pleasure in reading philosophical authors. In later years I denied myself the great pleasure of Nietzsche's works, with the conscious motive of not wishing to be hindered in the working out of my psychoanalytic impressions by any preconceived ideas. Therefore, I had to be prepared—and am so gladly—to renounce all claim to priority in those many cases in which the laborious psychoanalytic investigation can only confirm the insights intuitively won by the philosophers.

The theory of repression is the main pillar upon which rests the edifice of psychoanalysis. It is really the most essential part of it, and is itself nothing other than the theoretical expression of an experience which can be repeated at pleasure whenever one analyzes a neurotic patient without the aid of hypnosis. One is then confronted with a resistance which opposes the analytic work by causing a failure of memory in order to block it. This resistance had to be covered by the use of hypnosis; hence the history of psychoanalysis proper only starts technically with the rejection of hypnosis. The theoretical value of the fact that this resistance is connected with an amnesia leads unavoidably to that conception of the unconscious psychic activities which is peculiar to psychoanalysis, and distinguishes it markedly from the philosophical speculations about the unconscious. It may, therefore, be said that the psychoanalytic theory endeavors to explain two experiences, which result in a striking and unexpected manner during the attempt to trace back the morbid symptoms of a neurotic to their source in his life-history; viz., the facts of transference and of resistance. Every investigation which recognizes these two facts and makes them the starting points of its work may call itself psychoanalysis, even if it lead to

[3] Zentralblatt für Psychoanalyse, 1911, Vol. 1, p. 69.

other results than my own. But whoever takes up other sides of the problem and deviates from these two assumptions will hardly escape the charge of interfering with the rights of ownership through attempted imitation, if he insist upon calling himself a psychoanalyst.'

I would very energetically oppose any attempt to count the principles of repression and resistance as mere assumptions instead of results of psychoanalysis. Such assumptions of a general psychological and biological nature exist, and it would be quite to the point to deal with them in another place. The principle of repression, however, is an acquisition of the psychoanalytic work, won by legitimate means, as a theoretical extract from very numerous experiences. Just such an acquisition, but of much later days, is the theory of the infantile sexuality, of which no count was taken during the first years of tentative analytic investigation. At first it was only noticed that the effect of actual impressions had to be traced back to the past. However, "the seeker often found more than he bargained for." He was tempted always further back into this past and finally hoped to be permitted to tarry in the period of puberty, the epoch of the traditional awakening of the sexual impulses. His hopes were in vain. The tracks led still further back into childhood and into its earliest years. In the process of this work it became almost fatal for this young science. Under the influence of the traumatic theory of hysteria, following Charcot, one was easily inclined to regard as real and as of etiological importance the accounts of patients who traced back their symptoms to passive sexual occurrences in the first years of childhood, that is to say, speaking plainly, to seductions. When this etiology broke down through its own unlikelihood, and through the contradiction of well-established circumstances, there followed a period of absolute helplessness. The analysis had led by the correct path to such infantile sexual traumas, and yet these were not true. Thus the basis of reality had been lost. At that time I would gladly have let the whole thing slide, as did my respected forerunner Breuer, when he made his unwished-for discovery. Perhaps I persevered only because I had no longer any choice of beginning something else. Finally I reflected that, after all, no one has a right to despair if he has been disappointed only in his expectations. He merely needs to review them. If hysterics refer their symptoms to imaginary traumas, then this new fact signifies that they create such scenes in their phantasies, and hence psychic reality deserves to be given a place next to actual reality. This was soon followed by the conviction that these phantasies serve to hide the autoerotic activities of the early years of childhood, to idealize them and place them on a higher level, and now the whole sexual life of the child made its appearance behind these phantasies.

In this sexual activity of the first years of childhood, the concomitant constitution could finally attain its rights. Disposition and experience here became associated into an inseparable etiological unity, in that the disposition raised certain impressions to inciting and fixed traumas, which otherwise would have remained altogether banal and ineffectual, whilst the experiences evoked factors from the disposition which, without them, would have continued to remain dormant, and, perhaps, undeveloped. The last word in the question of traumatic etiology was later on said by Abraham, when he drew attention to the fact that just the peculiar nature of the child's sexual constitution enables it to provoke sexual experiences of a peculiar kind, that is to say, traumas.

My formulations concerning the sexuality of the child were founded at first almost exclusively on the results of the analyses of adults, which led back into the past. I was lacking in opportunity for direct observation of the child. It was, therefore, an extraordinary triumph when, years later, my discoveries were successfully confirmed for the greater part by direct observation and analyses of children of very early years, a triumph that appeared less and less on reflecting that the discovery was of such a nature that one really ought to be ashamed of having made it. The deeper one penetrated into the observation of the child, the more self-evident this fact seemed, and the more strange, too, became the circumstances that such pains had been taken to overlook it.

To be sure, so certain a conviction of the existence and significance of the infantile sexuality can be obtained only, if one follows the path of analysis, if one goes back from the symptoms and peculiarities of neurotics to their uttermost sources, the discovery of which explains what is explainable in them, and permits of modifying what can be changed. I understand that one can arrive at different conclusions if, as was recently done by C. G. Jung, one first forms for one's self a theoretical conception of the nature of the sexual impulse and thereby tries to understand the life of the child. Such a conception can only be chosen arbitrarily or with regard to secondary considerations, and is in danger of becoming inadequate to the sphere in which it was to be utilized. Doubtless, the analytic way also leads to certain final difficulties and obscurities in regard to sexuality and its relation to the whole life of the individual; but these cannot be set aside by speculations, and must wait till solutions will be found by means of other observations or of observations in other spheres.

I shall briefly discuss the history of dream-interpretation. This came to me as the first-fruits of the technical innovation, after, following a dim presentiment, I had decided to replace hypnosis with free associations. It was not the understanding of dreams towards which my curiosity was originally directed. I do not know of any influences which had guided my interest to this or inspired me with any helpful expectations. Before the cessation of my intercourse with Breuer I hardly had time to tell him, in so many words, that I now knew how to translate dreams. During the development of these discoveries the symbolism of the language of dreams was about the last thing which became known to me, since, for the understanding of symbols, the associations of the dreamer offer but little help. As I have held fast to the habit of first studying things themselves, before looking them up in books, I was able to ascertain for myself the symbolism of dreams before I was directed to it by the work of Sherner. Only later I came to value fully this means of expression of dreams. This was partly due to the influence of the works of Steckel, who was at first very meritorious but who later became most perfunctory. The close connection between the psychoanalytic interpretation of dreams and the once so highly esteemed art of dream interpretation of the ancients only became clear to me many years afterwards. The most characteristic and significant portion of my dream theory, namely, the reduction of the dream distortion to an inner conflict, to a sort of inner dishonesty, I found later in an author to whom medicine but not philosophy is unknown. I refer to the engineer J. Popper, who had published " Phantasies of a Realist" under the name of Lynkeus.

The interpretation of dreams became for me a solace and support in those difficult first years of analysis, when I had to master at the same time the technique, the clinic and the therapy of the neuroses, when I stood entirely alone, and in the confusion of problems and the accumulation of difficulties I often feared to lose my orientation and my confidence. It often took a long time before the proof of my assumption, that a neurosis must become comprehensible through analysis, was seen by the perplexed patient, but the dreams, which might be regarded as analogous to the symptoms, almost regularly confirmed this assumption.

Only because of these successes was I in condition to persevere. I have, therefore, acquired the habit of measuring the grasp of a psychological worker by his attitude to the problem of dream interpretation, and I have noticed, with satisfaction, that most of the opponents of psychoanalysis avoided this field altogether, or if they ventured into it, they behaved most awkwardly. The analysis of myself, the need of which soon became apparent to me, I carried out by the aid of a series of my own dreams which led me through all the happenings of my childhood years. Even today I am of the opinion that in the case of a prolific dreamer and a person not too abnormal, this sort of analysis may be sufficient.

By unfurling this developmental history, I believe I have shown what psychoanalysis is, better than I could have done by a systematic presentation of the subject. The special nature of my findings I did not then recognize. I sacrificed, unhesitatingly, my budding popularity as a physician and an extensive practice among nervous patients, because I searched directly for the sexual origin of their neuroses. In this way I gained a number of experiences which definitely confirmed my conviction of the practical significance of the sexual factor. Without any apprehension, I appeared as speaker at the Vienna Neurological Society, then under the presidency of Krafft-Ebing, expecting to be compensated, by the interest and recognition of my colleagues, for my own voluntary sacrifices. I treated my discoveries as indifferent contributions to science and hoped that others would treat them in the same way. Only the silence that followed my lectures, the space that formed about my person, and the insinuations directed towards me caused me to realize, gradually, that statements about the part played by sexuality in the etiology of the neuroses cannot hope to be treated like other communications. I realized that from then on I would belong to those who, according to Hebbel's expression, "have disturbed the world's sleep," and that I could not count upon being treated objectively and with toleration. But as my conviction of the average correctness of my observations and the conclusions grew greater and greater, and as my faith in my own judgment was not small, any more than was my moral courage, there could be no doubt as to the issue of this situation. I decided to believe that it fell to my lot to discover particularly significant associations, and felt prepared to bear the fate which sometimes accompanies such discoveries.

This fate I pictured to myself in the following manner. I would probably succeed in sustaining myself through the therapeutic successes of the new treatment, but science would take no notice of me in my lifetime. Some decades later, another would surely stumble upon the same, now untimely things, compel their recognition and thus bring me to honor as a necessarily unfortunate forerunner. Meantime I arrayed myself as comfortably as possible à la Robinson Crusoe upon my lonely island. When I look back to those lonely years, from the perplexities and vexatiousness of the present, it seems to me it was a beautiful and heroic time. The "splendid isolation" did not lack its privileges and charms. I did not need to read any literature nor to listen to badly informed opponents. I was subject to no influences, and no pressure was brought to bear on me. I learned to restrain speculative tendencies and, following the unforgotten advice of my master, Charcot, I looked at the same things again and often until they began of themselves to tell me something. My publications, for which I found shelter despite some difficulty, could safely remain far behind my state of knowledge. They could be delayed as long as I pleased, as there was no doubtful "priority" to be defended. "The Interpretation of Dreams," for example, was completed in all essentials in the beginning of 1896, but was written down only in 1899. The treatment of "Dora" was finished at the end of 1899. The history of her illness was completed in the next two weeks, but was only published in 1905. Meantime my writings were not in the reviewed professional literature of the day. If an exception was made they were always treated with scornful or pitying condescension. Sometimes a colleague would refer to me in one of his publications in very short and unflattering terms, such as " unbalanced," " extreme," or "very odd." It happened once that an assistant at the clinic in Vienna asked me for permission to attend one of my lecture courses. He listened devoutly and said nothing, but after the last lecture he offered to accompany me. During this walk he disclosed to me that, with the knowledge of his chief, he had written a book against my teachings, but he expressed much regret that he had only come to know these teachings better through my lectures. Had he known these before, he would have written very differently. Indeed, he had inquired at the clinic if he had not better first read " The Interpretation of Dreams," but had been advised against doing so, as it was not worth the trouble. As he now understood it, he compared my system of instruction with the Catholic Church. In the interests of his soul's salvation I will assume that this remark contained a bit of sincere recognition. But he ended by saying that it was too late to alter anything in his book as it was already printed. This particular colleague did not consider it necessary later on to tell the world something of the change in his opinions concerning my psychoanalysis. On the contrary, as permanent reviewer of a medical journal he showed a preference to follow its development with his hardly serious comments.

Whatever I possessed of personal sensitiveness was blunted in those years, to my advantage. But I was saved from becoming embittered by a circumstance that does not come to the assistance of all lonely discoverers. Such a one usually frets himself to find out the cause of the lack of sympathy or of the rejection he receives from his contemporaries, and perceives them as a painful contradiction against the certainty of his own conviction. That did not trouble me, for the psychoanalytic fundamental principles enabled me to understand this attitude of my environment as a necessary sequence. If it was true that the associations discovered by me were kept from the knowledge of the patient by inner affective resistances, then this resistance must manifest itself also in normal persons as soon as the repressed material is conveyed to them from the outside. It was not strange that these latter knew how to give intellectual reasons for their affective rejections of my ideas. This happened just as often with the patients, and the arguments advanced—arguments are as common as blackberries, to borrow from Falstaff's speech—were the same and not exactly brilliant. The only difference was that in the case of patients one had the means of bringing pressure to bear, in order to help them recognize and overcome their resistances, but in the case of those seemingly normal, such help had to be omitted. To force these normal people to a cool and scientifically objective examination of the subject was an unsolved problem, the solution of which was best left to time. In the history of science it has often been possible to verify that the very assertion which, at first, called forth only opposition, received recognition a little later without the necessity of bringing forward any new proofs.

That I have not developed any particular respect for the opinion of the world or any desire for intellectual deference during those years, when I alone represented psychoanalysis, will surprise no one.

II

Beginning with the year 1902 a number of young doctors crowded about me with the expressed intention to learn psychoanalysis, to practice it and to spread it. The impetus for this came from a colleague who had himself experienced the beneficial effects of the analytic therapy. We met on certain evenings at my residence, and discussed subjects according to certain rules. The visitors endeavored to orient themselves in this strange and new realm of investigation, and to interest others in the matter. One day a young graduate of the technical school found admission to our circle by means of a manuscript which showed extraordinary sense. We induced him to go through college and enter the university, and then devote himself to the non-medical application of psychoanalysis. Thus the little society gained a zealous and reliable secretary, and I acquired in Otto Rank a most faithful helper and collaborator.

Soon the little circle expanded, and in the course of the next few years changed a good deal in its composition. On the whole, I could flatter myself that in the wealth and variety of talent our circle was hardly inferior to the staff of any clinical teacher. From the very beginning it included those men who later were to play a considerable, if not always a delectable, part in the history of the psychoanalytic movement. But these developments could not have been guessed at that time. I was satisfied, and I believe I did all I could, to convey to the others what I knew and had experienced. There were only two inauspicious circumstances which at least mentally estranged me from this circle. I could not succeed in establishing among the members that friendly relation which should obtain among men doing the same difficult work, nor could I crush out the quarrels about the priority of discoveries, for which there were ample opportunities in those conditions of working together. The difficulties of teaching the practise of psychoanalysis, which are particularly great, and are often to blame for the present rejection of psychoanalysis, already made themselves felt in this Viennese private psychoanalytic society. I myself did not dare to present an as yet incomplete tech‑ nique, and a theory still in the making, with that authority which might have spared the others many a blind alley and many a final tripping up. The self-dependence of mental workers, their early independence of the teacher, is always gratifying psychologically, but it can only result in a scientific gain when during these labors certain, not too frequently occurring, personal relations are also ful‑ filled. Psychoanalysis particularly should have required a long and severe discipline and training of self-control. On account of the courage displayed in devotion to so ridiculed and fruitless a subject, I was inclined to tolerate among the members much to which otherwise I would have objected. Besides, the circle included not only physicians, but other cultured men who had recognized something significant in psychoanalysis. There were authors, ar‑ tists, and so forth. The "Interpretation of Dreams," the book on "Wit," and other writings, had already shown that the principles of psychoanalysis cannot remain limited to the medical field, but are capable of application to various other mental sciences.

In 1907 the situation suddenly altered and quite contrary to all expectations; it became evident that psychoanalysis had unobtru‑ sively awakened some interest and gained some friends, that there were even some scientific workers who were prepared to admit their allegiance. A communication from Bleuler had already acquainted me with the fact that my works were studied and applied in Burg‑ hölzli.[4] In January, 1907, the first man attached to the Zürich Clinic, Dr. Eitingon, visited me at Vienna. Other visitors soon followed, thus causing a lively exchange of ideas. Finally, by invitation of C. G. Jung, then still an assistant physician at Burghölzli, the first meeting took place at Salzburg, in the spring of 1908, where the friends of psychoanalysis from Vienna, Zürich, and other places met together. The result of this first psychoanalytic congress, was the founding of a periodical, which began to appear in 1909, under the name of "Jahrbuch für Psychoanalytische und Psychopatholo-

4 The Clinic of Psychiatry, Zürich.

•

gische Forschungen," published by Bleuler and Freud, and edited by Jung. An intimate comradeship in the work done at Vienna and Zürich found its expression in this publication.

I have repeatedly and gratefully acknowledged the efforts of the Zürich Psychiatric School in the spreading of psychoanalysis, especially those of Bleuler and Jung, and I do not hesitate to do the same today, even under such changed circumstances. It was certainly not the partisanship of the Zürich School which at that time first directed the attention of the scientific world to the subject of psychoanalysis. This latency period had just come to an end, and psychoanalysis everywhere became the object of constantly increasing interest. But whilst in all the other places this manifestation of interest resulted first in nothing but a violent and emphatic repudiation of the subject, in Zürich, on the contrary, the main feeling of the situation was that of agreement. In no other place was so compact a little gathering of adherents to be found, nowhere also was it possible to place a public clinic at the service of psychoanalytic investigation, or to find a clinical teacher who regarded the principles of psychoanalysis as an integral part of the teaching of psychiatry. The Zürich doctors became, as it were, the nucleus of the little band which was fighting for the recognition of psychoanalysis. Only in Zürich was there a possible opportunity to learn the new art and to apply it in practice. Most of my present-day followers and co-workers came to me via Zürich, even those who might have found, geographically speaking, a shorter road to Vienna than to Switzerland. Vienna lies in an eccentric position from western Europe, which houses the great centers of our culture. For many years it has been much affected by weighty prejudices. The representatives of the most prominent nations stream into Switzerland, which is so mentally active, and an infective lesion in this place was sure to become very important for the dissemination of the "psychic epidemic," as Hoche of Freiburg called it.

According to the testimony of a colleague who was an eyewitness of the developments at Burghölzli, it may be asserted that psychoanalysis awakened an interest there very early. Already in Jung's work on occult phenomena, published in 1902, there was an allusion to dream-interpretation. Ever since 1903 or 1904, according to my informer, psychoanalysis came into prominence. After the establment of personal relations between Vienna and Zürich, a society was also founded in Burghölzli in 1907 which discussed the problems of psychoanalysis at regular meetings. In the bond that united the Vienna and Zürich schools, the Swiss were by no means the merely recipient part. They had themselves already performed respectable scientific work, the results of which were of much use to psychoanalysis. The association-experiment, started by the Wundt School, had been interpreted by them in the psychoanalytic sense and had proved itself of unexpected usefulness. Thus it had become possible to get rapid experimental confirmation of psychoanalytic facts, and to demonstrate experimentally to beginners certain relationships which the analyst could only have talked about otherwise. The first bridge leading from experimental psychology to psychoanalysis had thus been constructed.

In psychoanalytic treatment, however, the association-experiment enables one to make only a preliminary, qualitative analysis of the case, it offers no essential contribution to the technique, and is really not indispensable in the work of analysis. Of more importance, however, was another discovery of the Zürich School, or rather, of its two leaders, Bleuler and Jung. The former pointed out that a great many purely psychiatric cases can be explained by the same psychoanalytic process as those used in dreams and in the neuroses (Freudsche Mechanismen). Jung employed with success the analytic method of interpretation in the strangest and most obscure phenomena of dementia præcox, the origin of which appeared quite clear when correlated with the life and interests of the patient. From that time on it became impossible for the psychiatrists to ignore psychoanalysis. Bleuler's great work on Schizophrenie (1911), in which the psychoanalytic points of view are placed on an equal footing with the clinical-systematic ones, brought this success to completion.

I must not omit to point out a divergence which was then already distinctly noticeable in the working tendencies of the two schools. Already in 1897 I had published the analysis of a case of schizophrenia, which showed, however, paranoid trends, so that its solution could not have anticipated the impression of Jung's analyses. But to me the important element had not been the interpretation of the symptoms, but rather the psychic mechanisms of the disease, and above all, the agreement of this mechanism with the one already known in hysteria. No light had been thrown at that time on the difference between these two maladies. I was then already working toward a theory of the libido in the neuroses which was to explain all neurotic as well as psychotic appearances on the basis of abnormal drifts of the libido. The Swiss investigators lacked this point of view. So far as I know Bleuler, even today, adheres to an organie causation for the forms of Dementia Præcox, and Jung, whose book on this malady appeared in 1907, upheld the toxic theory of the same at the Congress at Salzburg in 1908, which though not excluding it, goes far beyond the libido theory. On this same point he came to grief later (1912), in that he now used too much of the stuff which previously he refused to employ at all.

A third contribution from the Swiss School, which is to be ascribed probably entirely to Jung, I do not value as highly as do others who are not in as close contact with it. I speak of the theory of the *complexes*, which grew out of the "Diagnostische Assoziationsstudien" (1906–1910). It itself has neither resulted in a psychological theory nor has it added an unconstrained insertion to the context of the psychoanalytic principles. On the other hand, the word "complex" has gained for itself the right of citizenship in psychoanalysis, as being a convenient and often an indispensable term for descriptive summaries of psychologic facts. None other among the names and designations, newly coined as a result of psychoanalytic needs, has attained such widespread popularity; but no other term has been so misapplied to the detriment of clear thinking. In psychoanalytic diction one often spoke of the "return of the complex" when "the return of the repression" was intended to be conveyed, or one became accustomed to say "I have a complex against him," when more correctly he should have said "a resistance."

In the years after 1907, which followed the union of the schools of Vienna and Zürich, psychoanalysis received that extraordinary impetus in which it still finds itself today. This is positively attested by the spread of psychoanalytic literature and the increase in the number of doctors who desire to practice or learn it, also by the mass of attacks upon it by congresses and learned societies. It has wandered into the most distant countries, it everywhere shocked psychiatrists, and has gained the attention of the cultured laity and workers in other scientific fields. Havelock Ellis, who has followed its development with sympathy without ever calling himself its adherent, wrote, in 1911, in a paper for the Australasian Medical Congress: "Freud's psychoanalysis is now championed and carried out not only in Austria and in Switzerland, but in the United States, in England, India, Canada, and, I doubt not, in Australasia."[5] A doctor from Chile (probably a German) appeared at the International Congress in Buenos Ayres, in 1910, and spoke on behalf of the existence of infantile sexuality and praised the results of psychoanalytic therapy in obsessions.[6] An English neurologist in Central India informed me through a distinguished colleague who came to Europe, that the cases of Mohammedan Indians on whom he had practiced analysis showed no other etiology of their neuroses than our European patients.

The introduction of psychoanalysis into North America took place under particularly glorious auspices. In the autumn of 1909, Jung and myself were invited by President Stanley Hall, of Clark University, to take part in the celebration of the twentieth anniversary of the opening of Clark University, by giving some lectures in German. We found, to our great astonishment, that the unprejudiced men of that small but respected pedagogic-philosophical university knew all the psychoanalytic writings and had honored them

[5] Havelock Ellis, "The Doctrines of the Freudian School."

[6] G. Greve, "Sobre Psicologia y Psicoterapia de ciertos Estados angus. tiosos." See Zentralblatt für Psychoanalyse, Vol. 1, p. 594.

in their lectures to their students. Thus even in prudish America one could, at least in academic circles, discuss freely and treat scientifically all those things that are regarded as offensive in life. The five lectures that I improvised at Worcester then appeared in English in the American Journal of Psychology; later on they were printed in German under the title, "Über Psychoanalyse." Jung lectured on diagnostic association studies and on "conflicts in the psychic life of the child." We were rewarded for it with the honorary degree of LL.D. During this week of celebration at Worcester, psychoanalysis was represented by five persons. Besides Jung and myself there were Ferenczi, who had joined me as travelling-companion, Ernest Jones, then of Toronto University (Canada), now in London, and A. A. Brill, who was already practising psychoanalysis in New York.

The most noteworthy personal relationship which resulted at Worcester, was that established with James J. Putnam, teacher of neuropathology at Harvard University. For years he had expressed a disparaging opinion of psychoanalysis, but now he befriended it and recommended it to his countrymen and his colleagues in numerous lectures, rich in content and fine of form. The respect which he enjoys in America, owing to his character, his high moral standard and his keen love for truth, was very helpful to the cause of psychoanalysis and protected it against the denunciations to which it might otherwise have early succumbed. Yielding too much to the great ethical and philosophic bent of his nature Putnam later required of psychoanalysis what, to me, seems an impossible demand. He wished that it should be pressed into the service of a certain moral philosophical conception of the universe; but Putnam has remained the chief prop of the psychoanalytic movement in his native land.

For the diffusion of this movement Brill and Jones deserve the greatest credit. With a self-denying industry they constantly brought under the notice of their countrymen, through their works, the easily observable fundamental principles of psychoanalysis of everyday life, of the dream and of the neuroses. Brill has strengthened these influences by his medical activities and his translations of my writings: Jones, by illuminating lectures and clever discussions at the American Congresses.[7] The lack of a rooted scientific tradition and the lesser rigidity of official authority have been of decided advantage to the impetus given to psychoanalysis in America by Stanley Hall. It was characteristic there from the beginning that professors, heads of insane asylums, as well as independent practitioners, all showed themselves equally interested in psychoanalysis. But just for this very reason it is clear that the fight for psychoanalysis must be fought to a decisive end, where the greater resistance has been met with, namely, in the countries of the old cultural centers.

Of the European countries, France has so far shown herself the least receptive towards psychoanalysis, although creditable writings by the Zürich physician, A. Maeder, have opened up for the French reader an easy path to its principles. The first indications of interest came from provincial France. Moricheau-Beauchant (Poitiers) was the first Frenchman who openly accepted psychoanalysis. Régis and Hesnard (Bordeaux) have lately tried (1913) to overcome the prejudices of their countrymen by an exhaustive and senseful presentation of the subject, which takes exception only to symbolism. In Paris itself there still appears to reign the conviction (given such oratorical expression at London Congress 1913 by Janet) that every thing good in psychoanalysis only repeats, with slight modifications, the views of Janet—everything else in psychoanalysis being bad. Janet himself had to stand at this Congress a number of corrections from Ernest Jones, who was able to reproach him for his lack of knowledge of the subject. We cannot, however, forget the credit due Janet for his works on the psychology of the neuroses, although we must repudiate his claims.

Italy, after many promising starts, ceased to take further interest. Owing to personal connections psychoanalysis gained an early hearing in Holland: Van Emden, Van Ophuijsen, Van Renterghem

[7] The collected publications of these two authors have appeared in book form: Brill, "Psychoanalysis, its Theories and Practical Applications," 1912, 2d edition, 1914, Saunders, Philadelphia, and E. Jones's "Papers on Psychoanalysis," 1913, Wood and Company, New York.

("Freud en zijn school") and the two doctors Stärke are busy in Holland particularly on the theoretical side.[8] The interest in psychoanalysis in scientific circles in England developed very slowly, but the indications are that just here, favored by the English liking for the practical and their passionate championship of justice, a flourishing future awaits psychoanalysis.

In Sweden, P. Bjerre, successor to Wetterstand, has, at least temporarily, given up hypnotic suggestion in favor of analytic treatment. A. Vogt (Christiania) honored psychoanalysis already in 1907 in his "Psykiatriens gruntraek," so that the first text-book on psychiatry that took any notice of psychoanalysis was written in Norwegian. In Russia, psychoanalysis is very generally known and widespread; almost all my writings as well as those of other advocates of analysis are translated into Russian. But a deeper grasp of the analytic teaching has not yet shown itself in Russia. The contributions written by Russian physicians and psychiatrists are not at present noteworthy. Only Odessa possesses a trained psychoanalyst in the person of M. Wulff. The introduction of psychoanalysis into the science and literature of Poland is due chiefly to the endeavors of L. Jekels. Hungary, geographically so near to Austria, scientifically so foreign to it, has given to psychoanalysis only one co-worker, S. Ferenczi, but such an one as is worth a whole society.

The standing of psychoanalysis in Germany can be described in no other way than to state that it is the cynosure of all scientific discussion, and evokes from physicians as well as from the laity, opinions of decided rejection, which, so far, have not come to an end, but which, on the contrary, are constantly renewed and strengthened. No official seat of learning has, so far, admitted psychoanalysis. Successful practitioners who apply it are few. Only a few institutions, such as that of Binswanger's in Kreuzlingen (on Swiss soil) and Marcinowski's in Holstein, have opened their doors to

[8] The first official recognition that psychoanalysis and dream interpretation received was extended to them by the Psychiatrist Jelgersma, rector of the University of Leyden, in his rectorship address February 1, 1914.

psychoanalysis. In the critical city of Berlin, we have K. Abraham, one of the most prominent representatives of psychoanalysis. He was formerly an assistant of Bleuler. One might wonder that this state of things has thus continued for a number of years without any change, if it was not known that the above account merely describes the superficial appearances. One must not overestimate the significance of the rejection of psychoanalysis by the official representatives of science, the heads of institutions, as well as their young following. It is easy to understand why the opponents loudly raise their voices whilst the followers, being intimidated, keep silent. Many of the latter, whose first contributions to analysis raised high expectations, later withdrew from the movement under the pressure of circumstances. But the movement itself strides ahead quietly. It is always gaining new supporters among psychiatrists and the laity. It constantly increases the number of readers of psychoanalytic literature and thus forces the opponents to a more violent attempt at defense. In the course of these years I have read, perhaps a dozen times, in the reports of the transactions of certain congresses and of meetings of scientific societies, or in reviews of certain publications, that psychoanalysis was now dead, that it was finally overcome and settled. The answer to all this would have to read like the telegram from Mark Twain to the newspaper that falsely announced his death: " The report of my death is grossly exaggerated." After each of these death-notices, psychoanalysis has gained new followers and co-workers and has created for itself new organs. Surely to be reported dead is an advance over being treated with dead silence!

Hand in hand with its territorial expansion just described psychoanalysis became enlarged with regard to its contents through its encroaching upon fields of knowledge outside of the study of the neuroses and psychiatry. I will not treat in detail the development of this part of our branch of science since this was excellently done by Rank and Sachs (in Löwenfeld's " Grenzfragen ")[9] which pre-

[9] An English translation has just appeared in the Nervous and Mental Disease Monograph Series, No. 23.

sents exhaustively just these achievements in the work of analysis. Besides, here everything is in inchoate form, hardly worked out, mostly only preliminary and sometimes only in the stage of an intention. Every honest thinker will find herein no grounds for reproach. There is a tremendous amount of problems for a small number of workers whose chief activity lies elsewhere, who are obliged to attack the special problems of the new science with only amateurish preparation. These workers hailing from the psychoanalytic field make no secret of their dilettantism, they only desire to be guides and temporary occupants of the places of those specialists to whom they recommend the analytic technique and principles until the latter are ready to take up this work themselves. That the results aimed at are, even now, not at all insignificant, is due partly to the fruitfulness of the psychoanalytic method, and partly to the circumstance that already there are a few investigators, who, without being physicians, have made the application of psychoanalysis to the mental sciences their lifework.

Most of these psychoanalytic applications can be traced, as is easily understood, to the impetus given by my early analytic works. The analytic examinations of nervous patients and neurotic manifestations of normal persons drove me to the assumption of psychological relationships which, most certainly, could not be limited only to that field. Thus analysis presented us not only with the explanation of pathological occurrences, but also showed us their connection with normal psychic life and uncovered undreamed-of relations between psychiatry and a variety of other sciences dealing with activities of mind. Thus certain typical dreams furnished the understanding of many myths and fairy tales. Riklin and Abraham followed this hint and began those investigations about myths which have found their completion in the works of Rank on Mythology, works which do full justice to all the requirements of the specialist. The prosecution of dream-symbology led to the very heart of the problems of mythology, folk-lore (Jones, Storfer) and of religious abstraction. At one of the psychoanalytic congresses the audience was deeply impressed when a student of Jung pointed out the similarity of the phantasy-formation of schizophrenics with the cosmogonies of primitive times and peoples. In a later elaboration, no longer free from objection yet very interesting, Jung made use of mytho-logical material in an attempt to harmonize the neurotic with re-ligious and mythological phantasies.

Another path led from the investigation of dreams to the anal-ysis of poetic creations, and finally to the analysis of authors and artists themselves. Very soon it was discovered that the dreams invented by writers stand in the same relation to anal-ysis as do genuine dreams.[10] The conception of the unconscious psychic activity enabled us to get the first glimpse into the nature of the poetic creativeness. The valuation of the emotional feelings which we were forced to recognize while studying the neuroses en-abled us to recognize the sources of artistic productions and brought up the problem as to how the artist reacts to those stimuli and with what means he disguises his reactions.[11] Most psychoanalysts with wide interests have furnished contributions from their works for the treatment of these problems, which are among the most attractive in the application of psychoanalysis. Naturally here also opposi-tion was not lacking from those who are not acquainted with anal-ysis, and expressed itself with the same lack of understanding and passionate rejection as on the native soil of psychoanalysis. For it was to be expected as a matter of course, that everywhere psycho-analysis penetrates, it would have to go through the same struggle with the natives. However, these attempted invasions have not yet stirred up interest in all fields which will, in the future, be open to them. Among the strictly scientific applications of analysis to lit-erature the deep work of Rank on the theme of incest easily ranks first. Its content is certain to evoke the greatest unpopularity. Philological and historical works on the basis of psychoanalysis are few, at present. I myself dared to venture to make the first at-

[10] Cf. " Der Wahn und die Träume " in W. Jensen's " Gradiva."

[11] Rank, " Der Künstler," analyses of poets by Sadger, Reik, and others, my little monograph on a Kindheitserinnerung des Leonardo da Vinci; also Abraham's " Analyses von Segantini."

tempt into the problems of the psychology of religion in 1910, when I compared religious ceremonials with neurotic ceremonials. In his work on the "piety of the Count of Zinzendorf," as well as in other contributions, the Rev. Dr. Pfister, of Zürich, has succeeded in tracing back religious zealotism to perverse eroticism. In the recent works of the Zürich School one is more likely to find that religion becomes injected into the analysis rather than rationally explained by it.

In my four essays on "Totem and Taboo"[12] I made the attempt to discuss the problems of race psychology by means of analysis. This should lead us directly to the origins of the most important institutions of our civilization, such as state regulations, morality, religion, as well as to the origins of the interdiction of incest and of conscience. To what extent the relations thus obtained will be proof to criticism cannot be determined today.

My book on Wit[13] furnished the first examples of the application of analytic thinking to esthetic themes. Everything else is still waiting for workers, who can expect a rich harvest in this very field. We are lacking here in workers from these respective specialties and in order to attract such, Hans Sachs founded in 1912, the journal Imago, edited by himself and Rank. Hitschmann and v. Winterstein made a beginning with the psychoanalytic elucidation of philosophical systems and personalities. The continuation and deeper treatment of the same is much to be desired.

The revolutionary findings of psychoanalysis concerning the psychic life of the child, the part played therein by sexual impulses (v. Hug-Helmuth) and the fate of such participation of sexuality which becomes useless for the purpose of propagation, naturally drew attention to pedagogics, and instigated the effort to push the analytical viewpoint into the foreground of this sphere. Recognition is due to the Rev. Pfister for having begun this application of analysis with honest enthusiasm, and for having brought it to the

[12] A translation is in preparation.
[13] Wit and Its Relation to the Unconscious, translated by A. A. Brill, Moffat, Yard & Co., New York.

notice of ministers and educators.[14]   He succeeded in winning over
a number of Swiss pedagogues as sympathizers in this work.   It is
said that some preferred to remain circumspectly in the background.
A portion of the Vienna analysts seem to have landed in their retreat
from psychoanalysis on a sort of medical pedagogy.   (Adler and
Furtmüller, "Heilen and Bilden," 1913.)

I have attempted in these incomplete suggestions to indicate the,
as yet, hardly visible wealth of associations which have sprung up
between medical psychoanalysis and other fields of science.   There
is material for the work of a whole generation of investigators and
I doubt not that this work will be done when once the resistance to
psychoanalysis as such has been overcome.[15]

To write the history of the resistances, I consider, at present,
both fruitless and inopportune.   It would not be very glorious for
the scientific men of our day.   But I will add at once that it has
never occurred to me to rail against the opponents of psychoanalysis
merely because they were opponents, not counting a few unworthy
individuals, fortune hunters and plunderers such as in time of war
are always found on both sides.   For I knew how to account for
the behavior of these opponents and had besides discovered that
psychoanalysis brings to light the worst in every man.   But I decided
not to answer my opponents and, so far as I had influence, to keep
others from polemics.   The value of public or literary discussions
seemed to me very doubtful under the particular conditions in which
the fight over psychoanalysis took place.   The value of majorities
at congresses or society meetings was certainly doubtful, and my
confidence in the honesty and distinction of my opponents was always slight.   Observation shows that only very few persons are
capable of remaining polite, not to speak of objective, in any scientific dispute, and the impression gained from a scientific quarrel was
always a horror to me.   Perhaps this attitude of mine has been mis-

[14] "Die Psychoanalytische Methode," 1913, Vol. 1 of the Pedagogium,
Meumann and Messner.   English Translation by Dr. C. R. Payne.   Moffat,
Yard & Co., N. Y.

[15] Cf. my two essays in Scientia, Vol. XIV, 1913, "Das Interesse an der
Psychoanalyse."

understood, perhaps I have been considered as good-natured or so intimidated that it was supposed no further consideration need be shown me.

This is a mistake. I can revile and rave as well as any other, but I am not able to render into literary form the expressions of the underlying affects and therefore I prefer to abstain entirely.

Perhaps in many respects it might have been better had I permitted free vent to my own passions and to those about me. We have all heard the interesting attempt at an explanation of the origin of psychoanalysis from its Viennese milieu. Janet did not scorn to make use of it as late as 1913, although, no doubt, he is proud of being a Parisian. This *aperçu* says that psychoanalysis, especially the assertion that the neuroses can be traced back to disturbances in the sexual life, could only have originated in a city like Vienna, in an atmosphere of sensuality and immorality not to be found in other cities, and that it thus represents only a reflection, the theoretical projection as it were, of these particular Viennese conditions. Well, I certainly am no local patriot, but this theory has always seemed to be especially nonsensical, so nonsensical that sometimes I was inclined to assume that the reproaching of the Vienna spirit was only a euphemistic substitution for another one which one did not care to bring up publicly. If the assumptions had been of the opposite kind, we might be inclined to listen. But even if we assume that there might be a city whose inhabitants have imposed upon themselves special sexual restrictions and at the same time show a peculiar tendency to severe neurotic maladies, then such a town might well furnish the soil on which some observer might get the idea of connecting these two facts and of deducting the one from the other. But neither assumption fits Vienna. The Viennese are neither more abstemious nor yet more nervous than dwellers in any other metropolis. Sex matters are a little freer, prudishness is less than in the cities of western and northern Europe that are so proud of their chastity. Our supposed observer would, more likely, be led astray by the particular conditions prevailing in Vienna than be enlightened as to the cause of the neuroses.

But Vienna has done everything possible to deny her share in the origin of psychoanalysis. Nowhere else is the inimical indifference of the learned and cultured circles so clearly evident to the psychoanalyst.

Perhaps I am somewhat to blame for this by my policy of avoiding widespread publicity. If I had caused psychoanalysis to occupy the medical societies of Vienna with noisy sessions, with an unloading of all passions, wherein all reproaches and invectives carried on the tongue or in the mind would have been expressed, then perhaps the ban against psychoanalysis might, by now, have been removed and its standing no longer might have been that of a stranger in its native city. As it is, the poet may be right when he makes Wallenstein say:

> "Yet this the Viennese will not forgive me,
> That I did them out of a spectacle."

The task to which I am unequal, namely, that of reproaching the opponents "suaviter in modo" for their injustice and arbitrariness, was taken up by Bleuler in 1911 and carried out in most honorable fashion in his work, "Freud's Psychoanalysis: a Defense and a Criticism." It would be so entirely natural for me to praise this work, critical in two directions, that I hasten to tell what there is in it I object to. This work appears to me to be still very partisan, too lenient to the mistakes of our opponents, and altogether too severe to the shortcomings of our followers. This characterization of it may explain why the opinion of a psychiatrist of such high standing, of such indubitable ability and independence, has not had greater influence on his colleagues. The author of "Affectivity" (1906) must not be surprised if the influence of a work is not determined by the value of its argument but by the tone of its affect. Another part of this influence—the one on the followers of psychoanalysis—Bleuler himself destroyed later on by bringing into prominence in 1913, in his "Criticism of the Freudian School," the obverse side of his attitude to psychoanalysis. Therein he takes away so much from the structure of the psychoanalytic principles that our opponents may well be satisfied with the assistance of this defender. It was not new arguments or better observations that served Bleuler as a guidance for these verdicts, but only the reference to his own knowledge, the inadequacy of which the author no longer admits as in his earlier writings. Here an almost irreparable loss seemed to threaten psychoanalysis. However, in his last utterance ("Die Kritiken der Schizophrenie," 1914) on the occasion of the attacks made upon him owing to his introduction of psychoanalysis into his book on " Schizophrenie," Bleuler rises to what he himself terms a " haughty presumption :" " But now I will assume a haughty presumption, I consider that the many psychologies to date have contributed mighty little to the explanation of the connection between psychogenetic symptoms and diseases, but that the deeper psychology (tiefen psychologie) furnishes us a part of the psychology still to be created, which the physician needs in order to understand his patients and to heal them rationally ; and I even believe that in my ' Schizophrenie' I have taken a very small step towards this." The first two assertions are surely correct, the latter may be an error.

Since by the " deeper psychology " psychoanalysis alone is to be understood, we may, for the present, remain satisfied with this admission.

III

> "Cut it short!
> On doomsday 'twon't be worth a farthing!"
>
> *Goethe.*

Two years after the first congress the second private congress of psychoanalysts took place at Nuremberg, March, 1910. During the interval, whilst I was still under the impression of the favorable reception in America, the growing hostility in Germany and the un-expected support through the acquisition of the Zürich School, I had conceived a project which I was able to carry out, at this second congress, with the help of my friend S. Ferenczi. I had in mind to organize the psychoanalytic movement, to transfer its center to Zürich, and place it under a head who would take care of its future. As this found much opposition among the adherents of psychoanal-ysis, I will explain my motives more fully. Thus I hope to justify myself, even if it turns out that my action was not a very wise one.

I judged that the association with Vienna was no recommenda-tion, but rather an obstacle for the new movement. A place like Zürich, in the heart of Europe, where an academic teacher had opened his institution to psychoanalysis, seemed to me much more promising. Moreover, I assumed that my own person was a second obstacle. The estimate put upon my personality was utterly con-fused by the favor or dislike from different factions. I was either compared to Darwin and Kepler or reviled as a paralytic. I, there-fore, desired to push into the background not only the city whence psychoanalysis emanated, but also my own personality. Further-more, I was no longer young, I saw a long road before me and I felt oppressed by the idea that it had fallen to my lot to become a leader in my advanced age. Yet I felt that there must be a leader. I knew only too well what mistakes lay in wait for him who would undertake the practice of psychoanalysis, and hoped that many of these might be avoided if we had an authority who was prepared to guide and admonish. Such authority naturally devolved upon me in view of the indisputable advantage of fifteen years' experience. It was now my desire to transfer this authority to a younger man who would, quite naturally, take my place on my death. I felt that this person could be only C. G. Jung, for Bleuler was of my own age. In favor of Jung was his conspicuous talents, the contributions he had already made to analysis, his independent position, and the impression of energy which his personality always made. He also seemed prepared to enter into friendly relations with me, and to give up, for my sake, certain race-prejudices which he had so far permitted himself to indulge. I had no notion then that in spite of the advantages enumerated, this was a very unfortunate choice; that it concerned a person who, incapable of tolerating the authority of another, was still less fitted to be himself an authority, one whose energy was devoted to the unscrupulous pursuit of his own interests.

The formation of an official organization I considered necessary because I feared the abuses to which psychoanalysis would be subjected, once it should achieve popularity. I felt that there should be a place that could give the dictum: "With all this nonsense, analysis has nothing to do; this is not psychoanalysis." It was decided that at the meeting of the local groups which together formed the international organization, instruction should be given how psychoanalysis should be practised, that physicians should be trained there and that the local society should, in a way, stand sponsor for them. It also appeared to me desirable that the adherents of psychoanalysis should meet for friendly intercourse and mutual support, inasmuch as official science had pronounced its great ban and boycott against physicians and institutions practising psychoanalysis.

This and nothing else I wished to attain by the founding of the "International Psychoanalytic Association." Perhaps it was more than could possibly be attained. Just as my opponents learned that it was not possible to stem the new movement, so I had to learn, by experience, that it would not permit itself to be led along the particular path which I had laid out for it. The motion made by

Ferenczi at Nuremberg was seconded. Jung was elected president, and Riklin was chosen as secretary. It was also decided to publish a corresponding journal through which the central association was "to foster and further the science of psychoanalysis as founded by Freud both as pure psychology, as well as in its application to medicine and the mental sciences, and to promote assistance among the members in all their efforts to acquire and to spread psychoanalytic knowledge." The members of the Vienna group alone firmly opposed the project with passionate excitement. Adler expressed his fear that "a censorship and limitation of scientific freedom" was intended. The Viennese finally gave in, after having gained their point that Zürich should not be raised to the center of the association, but that the center should be the home city of the president, who was to be elected for two years.

At this congress three local groups were constituted: one in Berlin under the chairmanship of Abraham, one in Zürich, whose chairman became the president of the central association, and one in Vienna, the chairmanship of which I relinquished to Adler. A fourth group, in Budapest, could not be formed until later. On account of illness Bleuler had been absent from the congress. Later be evinced considerable hesitation about entering the association and although he let himself be persuaded to do so by my personal representations, he resigned a short time afterwards owing to disagreements at Zürich. This severed the connection between the Zürich group and the Burghölzli institution.

Another result of the Nuremberg Congress was the founding of the Zentralblatt für Psychoanalyse, which caused a reconciliation between Adler and Stekel. It had originally been intended as an opposing tendency and was to win back for Vienna the hegemony threatened by the election of Jung. But when the two founders of the journal, under pressure of the difficulty of finding a publisher, assured me of their friendly intentions and as guarantee of their attitude gave me the right to veto, I accepted the editorship and worked vigorously for this new organ, the first number of which appeared in September, 1910.

I will not continue the history of the Psychoanalytic Congress. The third one took place at Weimar, September, 1911, and even surpassed the previous ones in spirit and scientific interest. J. J. Putnam, who was present at this meeting, later expressed in America his satisfaction and his respect for the " mental attitude" of those present and quoted words which I was supposed to have used in reference to the latter : " They have learned to endure a bit of truth." As a matter of fact any one who has attended scientific congresses must have received a lasting impression in favor of the Psychoanalytic Association. I myself had presided over two former congresses. I thought it best to give every lecturer ample time for his paper and left the discussions of these lectures to take place later as a sort of private exchange of ideas. Jung, who presided over the Weimar meeting, reëstablished the discussions after each lecture, which had not, however, proved disturbing at that time.

Two years later, in September, 1913, quite another picture was presented by the congress at Münich which is still vividly recalled by those who were present. It was presided over by Jung in an unamiable and incorrect fashion: the lecturers were limited as to time, and the discussion dwarfed the lectures. Through a malicious mood of chance the evil genius of Hoche had taken up his residence in the same house in which the analysts held their meetings. Hoche could easily have convinced himself that his characterization of these psychoanalysts, as a sect, blindly and meekly following their leader, was true ad absurdum. The fatiguing and unedifying proceedings ended in the reëlection of Jung as president of the International Psychoanalytic Association, which fact Jung accepted, although two fifths of those present refused him their support. We took leave from one another without feeling the need to meet again!

About the time of this third Congress the condition of the International Psychoanalytic Association was as follows: The local groups at Vienna, Berlin, and Zürich had constituted themselves already at the congress at Nuremberg in 1910. In May, 1911, a group, under the chairmanship of Dr. L. Seif, was added at Münich. In the same year the first American local group was formed under the chairman-

ship of A. A. Brill under the name of "The New York Psychoanalytic Society." At the Weimar Congress, the founding of a
second American group was authorized. This came into existence
during the next year as "The American Psychoanalytic Association." It included members from Canada and all America; Putnam was elected president, and Ernest Jones was made secretary.
Just before the congress at Münich in 1913, a local group was
founded at Budapest under the leadership of S. Ferenczi. Soon
afterwards Jones, who settled in London, founded the first English
group. The number of members of the eight groups then in existence could not, of course, furnish any standard for the computation
of the non-organized students and adherents of psychoanalysis.

The development of the periodical literature of psychoanalysis
is also worthy of a brief mention. The first periodical publications
serving the interests of analysis were the Schriften zur angewandten
Seelenkunden which have appeared irregularly since 1907 and have
reached the fifteenth volume.[15a] They published writings by Freud,
Riklin, Jung, Abraham, Rank, Sadger, Pfister, M. Graf, Jones, Storfer and Hug-Hellmuth. The founding of the Imago, to be mentioned
later, has somewhat lowered the value of this form of publication. After the meeting at Salzburg, 1908, the Jahrbuch für psychoanalytische
und psychopathologische Forschungen was founded, which appeared
under Jung's editorship for five years, and it has now reappeared
under new editorship and under the slightly changed title of Jahrbuch der Psychoanalyse. It no longer wishes to be as in former
years, merely an archive for collecting works of psychoanalytic
merit, but it wishes to justify its editorial task by taking due notice
of all occurrences and all endeavors in the field of psychoanalysis.
As mentioned before Das Zentralblatt für Psychoanalyse started by
Adler and Stekel after the founding of the "International Association" (Nuremberg, 1910) went through in a short time a very varied
career. Already in the tenth issue of the first volume there was an
announcement that in view of scientific difference of opinion with

[15a] Dreams and Myths, Wish-fulfillment and Fairy Tales, Myth of the
Birth of the Hero, in this series are translated in the Monograph Series.

the editors, Dr. Adler had decided voluntarily to withdraw his collaboration. This placed the entire editorship in the hands of Dr. Stekel (summer of 1911). At the Weimar congress the Zentralblatt was raised to the official organ of the "International Association" and by raising the annual dues it was made accessible to all members. Beginning with the third number of the second year (winter 1912) Stekel alone became responsible for the contents of the journal. His behavior, which is difficult to explain in public, forced me to sever all my connections with this journal and to give psychoanalysis in all haste a new organ, the International Journal for Medical Psychoanalysis (Internationale Zeitschrift für Ärztliche Psychoanalyse). With the help of almost all my collaborators and the new publisher, H. Heller, the first number of this new journal was able to appear in January, 1913, to take the place of the Zentralblatt as the official organ of the "International Psychoanalytic Association."

Meanwhile Dr. Hanns Sachs and Dr. Otto Rank founded early in 1912 a new journal, Imago (published by Heller), whose only aim is the application of psychoanalysis to mental sciences. Imago has now reached the middle of its third year, and enjoys the increasing interest of readers who are not medically interested in psychoanalysis.

Apart from these four periodical publications (Schriften z. Angew. Seelenkunde, Jahrbuch, Intern. Zeitschrift, and Imago) other German and foreign journals have contributed works that can claim a place in psychoanalytic literature. The Journal of Abnormal Psychology, published by Morton Prince, as a rule, contains many good analytical contributions. In the winter of 1913 Dr. White and Dr. Jelliffe started a journal exclusively devoted to psychoanalysis, THE PSYCHOANALYTIC REVIEW, which takes into account the fact that most physicians in America interested in psychoanalysis do not master the German language.

I am now obliged to speak of two secessions which have taken place among the followers of psychoanalysis. The first of these took place in the interval between the founding of the association

in 1910 and the congress at Weimar, 1911, the second took place
after this, and came to light in Münich in 1913. The disappoint-
ment which they caused me might have been avoided if more attention had been paid to the mechanisms of those who undergo analytical treatment. I was well aware that any one might take flight on
first approach to the unlovely truths of analysis; I myself had always
asserted that any one's understanding may be suspended by one's
own repressions (through the resistances which sustain them) so
that in his relation to psychoanalysis he cannot get beyond a certain
point. But I had not expected that any one who had mastered analysis to a certain depth could renounce this understanding and lose
it. And yet daily experience with patients had shown that the total
rejection of all knowledge gained through analysis may be brought
about by any deeper stratum of particularly strong resistance.
Even if we succeed through laborious work in causing such a patient
to grasp parts of analytic knowledge and handle these as his own
possessions, it may well happen that under the domination of the
next resistance he will throw to the winds all he has learned and
will defend himself as in his first days of treatment. I had to learn
that this can happen among psychoanalysts just as among patients
during treatment.

It is no enviable task to write the history of these two secessions,
partly because I am not impelled to it by strong personal motives—
I had not expected gratitude nor am I to any active degree revenge-
ful—and partly because I know that I hereby lay myself open to the
invectives of opponents manifesting but little consideration, and at
the same time I regale the enemies of psychoanalysis with the long
wished-for spectacle of seeing the psychoanalysts tearing each other
to pieces. I had to exercise much control to keep myself from fighting with the opponents of psychoanalysis, and now I feel constrained
to take up the fight with former followers or such as still wish to
be called so. I have no choice; to keep silent would be comfortable
or cowardly, but it would hurt the subject more than the frank un-
covering of the existing evils. Any one who has followed the
growth of scientific movements will know that quite similar dis-

turbances and dissensions took place in all of them. It may be that elsewhere they are more carefully concealed. However, psychoanalysis, which denies many conventional ideals, is also more honest in these things.

Another very palpable inconvenience lies in the fact that I cannot altogether avoid going into an analytic elucidation. Analysis is not, however, suitable for polemical use; it always presupposes the consent of the one analyzed and the situation of a superior and subordinate. Therefore he who wishes to use analysis with polemic intent must offer no objection if the person so analyzed will, in his turn, use analysis against him, and if the discussion merges into a state in which the awakening of a conviction in an impartial third party is entirely excluded. I shall, therefore, make here the smallest possible use of analysis, thereby limiting my indiscretion and aggression against my opponents, and I will also add that I base no scientific criticism on this means. I have nothing to do with the possible substance of truths in the theories to be rejected nor am I seeking to refute the same. This task may be left to other able workers in the field of psychoanalysis, and some of it has already been done. I only desire to show that these theories deny the basic principles of analysis—I will show in what points—and for this reason should not be known under this name. I shall, therefore, use analysis only to make clear how these deviations from analysis could take place among analysts. At the parting places I am, of course, obliged to defend the just rights of psychoanalysis with purely critical remarks.

Psychoanalysis has found as its first task the explanation of the neuroses; it has taken the two facts of resistance and transference as starting points, and by bearing in mind the third fact of amnesia in the theories of repression, it has given justification to the sexual motive forces of the neuroses and of the unconscious. Psychoanalysis has never claimed to give a perfect theory of the human psychic life, but has only demanded that its discoveries should be used for the completion and correction of knowledge we have gained elsewhere. But Alfred Adler's theory goes far beyond this goal. It pretends to explain with one stroke the behavior and character of men as well as their neurotic and psychotic maladies. As a matter of fact, Adler's theory is more adequate to any other field than to that of the neuroses, which he still puts in the first place because of the history of its origin. I had the opportunity of studying Dr. Adler many years and have never denied him the testimonial of having a superior mind, especially endowed speculatively. As proof of the "persecution" which he claims to have suffered at my hands, I can only say that after the formation of the Association I handed over to him the leadership of the Vienna group. It was only after urgent requests from all the members of the society that I could be prevailed upon to resume the presidency at the scientific proceedings. When I had recognized Dr. Adler's slight talent for the estimation of the unconscious material, I expected that he would know how to discover the connections between psychoanalysis and psychology and the biological bases of the impulses, a discovery to which he was entitled, in a certain sense, through his valuable studies about the inferiority of organs. He really did bring out some thing, but his work makes the impression as if—to speak in his own jargon—it were intended to prove that psychoanalysis was wrong in everything and that the significance of the sexual impelling forces could only be due to gullibility about the assertions of neurotics. Of the personal motive of his work I may also speak publicly, since he himself revealed it in the presence of a small circle of members of the Vienna group. "Do you believe," he remarked, "that it is such a great pleasure for me to stand in your shadow my whole life?" To be sure I see nothing objectionable in the fact that a younger man should frankly admit an ambition which one might, in any case, suspect as one of the incentives of his work. But even under the domination of such a motive a man should know how to avoid being "unfair" as designated by the English with their fine social tact. We Germans have only a much coarser word at our disposal to convey this idea. How little Adler has succeeded in not being unfair is shown by the great number of mean outbursts of anger which distort his writings, and by the feeling of an ungovernable mania for priority which pervades his work. At the Vienna Psychoanalytic Society we once heard him claim for himself the priority for the viewpoints of the "unity of the neuroses" and the "dynamic conception" of the same. This was a great surprise for me as I had always believed that I had represented these two principles before I had ever known Adler.[15b]

This striving of Adler for a place in the sun has brought about, however, one result, which must be considered beneficial to psychoanalysis. When I was obliged to bring about Adler's resignation from the editorial staff of the Zentralblatt, after the appearance of his irreconcilable scientific antagonisms, Adler also left the Vienna group and founded a new society to which he first gave the tasteful name "Society for Free Psychoanalysis." But the outside public, unacquainted with analysis, is evidently as little skilled in recognizing the difference between the views of two psychoanalysts, as are Europeans in recognizing the tints between two Chinese faces. The "free" psychoanalysis remained in the shadow of the "official" and "orthodox" one, and was treated only as an appendage of the latter. Then Adler took the step for which we are thankful. He severed all connection with psychoanalysis and named his teachings "The Individual Psychology." There is much space on God's earth, and any one who can is surely justified in tumbling about upon it uninhibited; but it is not desirable to continue living under one roof when people no longer understand one another and no longer get on together. Adler's "Individual Psychology" is now one of the many psychological movements opposed to psychoanalysis, and its further development lies outside our interests.

Adler's theory was, from the very beginning, a "system," which psychoanalysis was careful not to become. It is also an excellent example of a "secondary elaboration" as seen, for example, in the process which the waking thought produces in dream material.[16] In this case instead of dream material there is the material newly

15b Adler's Inferiority of Organs, translated by Jelliffe, appears as Monograph 24. His, "Nervous Character," translated by Glueck and Lind, published by Moffat, Yard & Co., N. Y.

16 Cf. The Interpretation of Dreams, p. 389, translated by A. A. Brill, The Macmillan Co., New York, and Allen, London.

acquired from the viewpoint of the ego and brought under the familiar categories of the same. It is then translated, changed, and as thoroughly misunderstood as happens in the case of dream-formation. Adler's theory is thus characterized less by what it asserts than by what it denies. It consequently consists of three elements of quite dissimilar value; first, good contributions to the psychology of the ego, which are superfluous but admissible; secondly, translations of analytical facts into the new jargon, and, thirdly, distortions and perversions of these facts when they do not fit into the ego presuppositions. The elements of the first kind have never been ignored by psychoanalysis, although it owed no special attention to them. Psychoanalysis had a greater interest in showing that all ego strivings are mixed with libidinous components. Adler's theory emphasizes the counterpart to it; namely, that all libidinous feeling contains an admixture of egotism. This would have been a palpable gain if Adler had not made use of this assertion to deny, every time, the libidinous feelings in favor of the impelling ego components. His theory thus does exactly what all patients do, and what our conscious thinking always does, it rationalizes, as Jones would say, in order to conceal the unconscious motives. Adler is so consistent in this, that he considers the object of evincing domination over the woman, to be on the top, as the mainspring of the sexual act. I do not know if he has upheld this monstrous idea in his writings.

Psychoanalysis early recognized that every neurotic symptom owes the possibility of its existence to some compromise. It must, therefore, also put to some good account the demands of the ego which manages the repression, it must offer it some advantages by finding for it some useful employment, otherwise it would suffer the same fate as the originally defended impulses. The term "morbid gain" expresses this state of affairs. One might even have been justified in differentiating the primary gain for the ego which must have been active at the origin, from a " secondary " gain which appears in connection with other intentions of the ego, when the symptom is about to assert itself. It has also long been known to analysis that the withdrawal of this morbid gain, or the cessation of the same in consequence of some real change, is one of the mechanisms in the cure of the symptom.   On these relationships which can be verified and understood without difficulty, Adler's theory puts the greatest emphasis.   It entirely overlooks the fact that innumerable times the ego makes a virtue out of necessity in submitting to the most undesired symptom forced upon it, because of the use it can make of it, e. g., when the ego accepts anxiety as a means of security.   Here the ego plays the absurd part of the Pierot in the circus, who, through his gestures, wishes to convey to the spectators the impression that all changes in the menage are taking place at his command.   But only the youngest among the spectators believe him.

For the second part of Adler's theory psychoanalysis must stand security as for its own possessions.   For it is nothing but psychoanalytic knowledge which the author had from all the sources opened to him during ten years of our joint work, but which he later marked as his own after changing the nomenclature.   For instance, I myself consider "security" a better word than "protective measure," which I used; but cannot find in it any new meaning. Similarly one will find in Adler's statements a great many long-known features if one will replace the expressions "feigned" (fingiert) fictive and fiction, by the original words "to fancy" and "phantasy."   This identity would be emphasized by psychoanalysis, even if the author had not for many years participated in our common work.

The third part of Adler's theory, which consists in giving new interpretations to, and in distorting the disagreeable facts of psychoanalysis, contains that which definitely severs the actual "Individual Psychology" from psychoanalysis.   As is known the principle of Adler's system states that it is the object of the self-assertion of the individual, his "will to power" in the form of the "masculine protest," to manifest itself domineeringly in the conduct of life, in character formation and in the neurosis.   This "masculine protest," the Adlerism motor, is nothing else, however, than the repression set free from its psychological mechanism, and what is more, it is sexualized and thus hardly in keeping with the vaunted expulsion of sexuality from its place in the psychic life. The "masculine protest" certainly exists, but in constituting it as the motor of the psychic life, observation has only played the part of the springboard which one leaves in order to uplift one's self. Let us consider one of the most fundamental situations of the infantile desire; namely, the observation of the sexual act between adults by the child. When the life-history of such persons is later subjected to analysis by a physician, it is found that at this moment the minor spectator was seized by two feelings; one, in the case of a boy, to put himself in the place of the active man, and the other, the opposing feeling, to identify himself with the suffering woman. Both strivings conjointly exhaust the pleasure that might have resulted from this situation. Only the first feeling can come under the head of the "masculine protest" if this idea is to retain any meaning at all. The second feeling, whose fate Adler either ignores or does not know, is really the one which assumes greater significance in the later neurosis. Adler has placed himself so entirely into the jealous confinement of the ego, that he only accounts for such emotional feelings as are agreeable to the ego and furthered by it; but the case of the neurosis, which opposes these strivings, lies beyond his horizon.

Adler's most serious deviations from the reality of observation and his deepest confusion of ideas have arisen in his attempt to correlate the basic principle of his theory with the psychic life of the child, an attempt which has become inevitable in psychoanalysis. The biological, social, and physiological meaning of "masculine" and "feminine" have here become mixed into a hopeless composition. It is quite impossible, and it can easily be disproved by observation, that the masculine or feminine child builds its plan of life on any original undervaluation of the feminine sex; nor is it conceivable that a child can take as the guiding line the wish: "I will be a real man." In the beginning no child has even an inkling of the significance of the difference in sex, more likely it starts with the assumption that both sexes possess the same (male) genital. It does not begin its sexual investigation with the problem of sex differentiation and is far from entertaining the social undervaluation of the woman. There are women in whose neurosis the wish to be a man never played any part. So far as the "masculine protest" is concerned, it can easily be traced back to a disturbance of the original narcissism caused by the threat of castration; that is, to the first hindrance of sexual activity. All dispute as to the psychogenesis of the neuroses must ultimately be decided in the sphere of the childhood neuroses. The careful analysis of a neurosis of the early years of childhood puts an end to all mistakes in regard to the etiology of the neuroses, and all doubts as to the part played by the sexual impulses. That is why Adler in his criticism of Jung's " Conflicts of the Child's Mind " was obliged to resort to the imputation that the material of the case surely must have followed a uniform new tendency " from the father."[17]

I will not linger any longer over the biological side of Adler's theory, and will not examine whether the palpable inferiority of organs or the subjective feeling of the same (one often cannot tell which) can possibly be the basis of Adler's system. Only permit me to remark that this would make the neurosis a by-product of the general stunting, while observation teaches that an excessively large number of hideous, misshapen, crippled, and wretched creatures have failed to react to their deficiencies by developing a neurosis. Nor will I consider the interesting information that the sense of inferiority goes back to infantile feelings. It shows us in what disguise the doctrine of infantilism, so much emphasized in psychoanalysis, returns in Adler's Individual Psychology. On the other hand, I am obliged to emphasize how all psychological acquisitions of psychoanalysis have been disregarded by Adler. In his book " The Nervous Character," the unconscious still appears as a psychological peculiarity, but without any relation to his system. Later, he declared, quite logically, that it was a matter of indifference to him whether any conception be conscious or unconscious. For the principle ·of repressions, Adler never evinced any understanding. While reviewing a lecture before the Vienna Society in 1911, he

[17] Zentralbl., Vol. I, p. 122. See "Analytical Psychology," Moffat, Yard & Co., N. Y.

said: "On the strength of a case I wish to point out that the patient had never repressed his libido, against which he continually tried to secure himself."[18]   Soon thereafter at a discussion in Vienna Adler said: "If you ask whence comes the repression, you are told: from culture. But if you ask whence comes culture, the reply is: from the repression. So you see it is only a question of a play on words." A small fragment of the sagacity used by Adler to defend his "nervous character" might have sufficed to show him the way out of this pettifogging argument. There is nothing mysterious about it, except that culture depends upon the acts of repression of former generations, and that each new generation is required to retain this culture by carrying out the same repressions. I have heard of a child that considered itself fooled and began to cry, because to the question: "Where do eggs come from?" it received the answer, "Eggs come from hens," and to the further question: "Where do the hens come from?" the information was "From the eggs," and yet this was not a play upon words. The child had been told what was true.

Just as deplorable and devoid of substance is all that Adler has said about the dream—that shibboleth of psychoanalysis. At first he considered the dream as a turning from the masculine to the feminine line, which simply means translating the theory of wish-fulfillment in dreams into the language of the "masculine protest." Later he found that the essence of the dream lies in the fact that it enables man to realize unconsciously what is denied him consciously. Adler should also be credited with the priority of confounding the dream with the latent dream-thoughts, on the cognition of which rests his idea of "prospective tendency." Maeder followed him in this, later on. In doing so he readily overlooks the fact that every interpretation of the dream which really tells nothing comprehensible in its manifest appearance rests upon the same dream-interpretation, whose assumptions and conclusions he is disputing. Concerning resistance Adler asserts that it serves to strengthen the patient against the physician. This is certainly correct. It means as much

[18] Korrespondenzbl., No. 5, Zurich, April, 1911.

as saying that it serves the resistance. But whence this resistance originates, and how it happens that its phenomena serve the patient's interest, these questions, as if of no interest for the ego, are not further discussed by Adler. The detailed mechanisms of symptoms and phenomena, the motivation of the variety of diseases and morbid manifestations, find no consideration at all with Adler, since everything is equally subservient to the "masculine protest," to the self-assertion, and to the exaltation of the personality. The system is finished, at the expense of an extraordinary labor of new interpretation, yet it has not contributed a single new observation. I believe that I have succeeded in showing that his system has nothing whatever in common with psychoanalysis.

The picture which one derives from Adler's system is founded entirely upon the impulse of aggression. It has no place at all for love. One might wonder that such a cheerless aspect of life should have received any notice whatever; but we must not forget that humanity, oppressed by its sexual needs, is prepared to accept anything, if only the "overcoming of sexuality" is held out as bait.

The secession of Adler's faction was finished before the Congress at Weimar which took place in 1911, while the one of the Swiss School began after this date. Strangely enough, the first indications of it were found in some remarks by Riklin in popular articles printed in Swiss literature, from which the general public learned, even before Riklin's closest colleagues, that psychoanalysis had succeeded in overcoming some regretable mistakes which discredited it. In 1912 Jung boasted, in a letter to me from America, that his modifications of psychoanalysis had overcome the resistances to it in many persons, who hitherto wanted to know nothing about it. I replied that this was nothing to boast about, that the more he sacrificed of the hard-won truths of psychoanalysis, the less resistances he would encounter. This modification for the introduction of which the Swiss are so proud, again was nothing more or less than the theoretical suppression of the sexual factor. I admit that from the very beginning I have regarded this "progress" as a too-far-reaching adaptation to the demands of actuality.

These two retrogressive movements, tending away from psycho-analysis, which I will now compare, also resemble each other in the fact that they are seeking to obtain a favorable opinion by means of certain lofty points of view, as *sub specie æternitatis*. In the case of Adler, this rôle is played by the relativity of all knowledge, and by the rights of the personality to construe artificially any piece of knowledge to suit the individual; while Jung insists on the cultural historical rights of youth to throw off any fetters that tyrannical old age with ossified views would forge for it. These arguments require some repudiation. The relativity of all our knowledge is a consideration which may be used as an argument against any other science besides psychoanalysis. This idea originates from well-known reactionary streams of the present day, inimical to science, and wishes to give the appearance of a superiority to which we are not entitled. Not one of us can guess what may be the ultimate judgment of mankind about our theoretical efforts. There are examples to show that what was rejected by the next three genera-tions was corrected by the fourth and its recognition thus brought about. There is nothing else for the individual to do than to defend, with all his strength, his conviction based on experience after he has carefully listened to his own criticisms and has given some atten-tion to the criticisms of his opponents. Let him be content to con-duct his affair honestly and not assume the office of judge, which is reserved for a remote future. To accentuate personal arbitrariness in scientific matters is bad; it evidently wishes to deny to psycho-analysis the value of a science, which, to be sure, Adler has already depreciated by the aforementioned remark. Any one who highly regards scientific thinking will rather seek for means and methods by which to restrict, if possible, the factor of personal and artificial arbitrariness wherever it still plays too large a part. Besides one must remember that all agitation in defending is out of place. Adler does not take these arguments seriously. They are only for use against his opponents, but they respect his own theories. They have not prevented Adler's own adherents from celebrating him as the Messiah, for whose appearance waiting humanity had been prepared

by so many forerunners.   The Messiah is surely no longer anything
relative.

Jung's argument *ad captandam benevolentiam* rests on the all-
too-optimistic assumption that the progress of humanity, of civilization, and of knowledge has always continued in an unbroken line,
as if there had never been any epigones, reactions, and restorations
after every revolution, as if there had never been races who, because
of a retrogression, had to renounce the gain of former generations.
The approach to the standpoint of the masses, the giving up of an
innovation that has proved unpopular, all these make it altogether
unlikely that Jung's correction of psychoanalysis could lay claim to
being a liberating act of youth.   Finally it is not the years of the
doer that decide it, but the character of the deed.

Of the two movements we have here considered, that headed by
Adler is undoubtedly the more important.   Though radically false,
it is, nevertheless, characterized by consistency and coherence and it
is still founded on the theory of the impulse.   On the other hand,
Jung's modification has lessened the connection between the phenomena and the impulses : besides, as its critics (Abraham, Ferenczi,
Jones) have already pointed out, it is so unintelligible, muddled, and
confused, that it is not easy to take any attitude towards it.   Wherever one touches it, one must be prepared to be told that one has
misunderstood it, and it is impossible to know how one can arrive at
a correct understanding of it.   It represents itself in a peculiarly
vacillating manner, since at one time it calls itself "a quite tame
deviation, not worthy of the row which has arisen about it" (Jung),
yet, at another time, it calls itself a new salvation with which a new
epoch shall begin for psychoanalysis, in fact, a new aspect of the
universe for everything else.

When one thinks of the disagreements between the individual
private and public expressions of Jung's utterances one is obliged to
ask to what extent this is due to his own lack of clearness and lack
of sincerity.   Yet, it must be admitted that the representatives of the
new theory find themselves in a difficult position.   They are now
disputing things which they themselves formerly defended and what

is more, this dispute is not based on new observations which might have taught them something fresh, but rather on a different interpretation which causes them to see things in a different light from that in which they saw them before. It is for this reason that they will not give up their connection with psychoanalysis as the representatives of which they first became known in the world. They prefer to proclaim that psychoanalysis has changed. At the Congress of Münich I was obliged to clear up this confusion and did so by declaring that I could not recognize the innovation of the Swiss School as a legitimate continuation and further development of the psychoanalysis which had originated with me. Outside critics (like Furtmüller) had already recognized this state of affairs and Abraham says, quite rightly, that Jung is in full retreat away from psychoanalysis. I am naturally entirely willing to admit that any one has the right to think and to write what he wishes, but he has not the right to make it out to be something different from what it really is.

Just as Adler's researches brought something new into psychoanalysis, a piece of the ego-psychology, and paid only too dearly for this gift by repudiating all the fundamental analytic principles, in the same way Jung and his adherents have based their fight against psychoanalysis upon a new contribution to the same. They have traced in detail (what Pfister did before them) how the material of the sexual ideas originating in the family complex and in the incestuous object selection can be used to represent the highest ethical and religious interests of mankind, that is, they have explained a remarkable case of sublimation of the erotic impelling forces and the transformation of the same into strivings that can no longer be called erotic. All this harmonized very well with the assumptions of psychoanalysis, and would have agreed very well with the conception that in the dream and in the neurosis one sees the regressive elucidations of these and all other sublimations. But the world would have exclaimed that ethics and religion had been sexualized. I cannot help assuming " finally " that the investigators found themselves quite unequal to the storm they had to face.

Perhaps the storm began to rage in their own bosoms. The previous theological history of so many of the Swiss workers is as important in their attitude to psychoanalysis as is the socialistic record of Adler for the development of his "psychology." One is reminded of Mark Twain's famous story about the fate of his watch and to the speculative remark with which he closed it: "And he used to wonder what became of all the unsuccessful tinkers, and gunsmiths, and shoemakers, and blacksmiths; but nobody could ever tell him."

I will encroach upon the realm of parables and will assume that in a certain society there lived a parvenu who boasted of descent from a very noble family not locally known. But it so happened that it was proved to him that his parents were living somewhere in the neighborhood and were very simple people, indeed. Only one way out remained to him and he seized upon it. He could no longer deny his parents, but he asserted that they were very aristocratic by origin but much come down in the world, and secured for them at some obliging office a document showing their descent. It seems to me that the Swiss workers had been obliged to act in a similar manner. If ethics and religion could not be sexualized, but must be regarded as something "higher" from the very beginning, and as their origin from the family and Œdipus complexes seemed undeniable, then there was only one way out; namely, that these complexes themselves, from the beginning, could not have the significance which they appeared to express, but must have that higher "anagogic" sense (to use Silberer's nomenclature) with which they adapt themselves for proper use in the abstract streams of thought of ethics and religious mysticism.

I am quite prepared to be told once more that I have misunderstood the contents and object of the theory of the New-Zürich School, but here wish to protest against being held responsible for those contradictions to my theories that have arisen as a result of the publications of this school. The burden of responsibility rests on them, not on me. In no other way can I make comprehensible to myself the ensemble of Jung's innovations or grasp them in their associations. All the changes which Jung has perpetrated upon psychoanalysis originated in the intention of setting aside all that is objectionable in the family complexes, in order that these objectionable features may not be found again in religion and ethics. The sexual libido was replaced by an abstract idea, of which it may be said that it remained equally mysterious and incomprehensible alike to fools and to the wise. The Œdipus-complex, we are told, has only a "symbolical" sense, the mother therein representing the unattainable which must be renounced in the interests of cultural development. The father who is killed in the Œdipus myth represents the "inner" father from whose influence we must free ourselves in order to become independent. No doubt other portions of the material of sexual conceptions will, in time, receive similarly new interpretations. In place of the conflict between erotic strivings adverse to the ego and the self-assertion, we are given the conflict between the "life-task" and the "psychic-laziness." The neurotic guilty conscience corresponds with the reproach of not having put to good account one's life-task. Thus a new religio-ethical system was founded which, exactly like Adler's, was obliged to give new interpretations, to distort or set aside the actual results of analysis. As a matter of fact they have caught a few cultural higher notes from the symphony of the world's by-gones, but once again have failed to hear the powerful melody of the impulses.

In order to hold this system together it was necessary to draw away entirely from the observations and technique of psychoanalysis. Now and then the enthusiasm for the higher cause even permits a total disregard for scientific logic, as for instance, when Jung maintains that the Œdipus complex is not "specific" enough for the etiology of the neuroses, and ascribed this specificity to laziness, that is, to the most universal quality of animate and inanimate bodies! Moreover, it is to be remarked that the "Œdipus complex" only represents a capacity on which the psychic forces of the individual measure themselves, and is not in itself a force, like the "psychic laziness." The study of the individual man has shown and always will show that the sexual complexes are alive in him in their original sense. That is why the study of the individual was pushed back by Jung and replaced by the judgment of the essential facts from the study of the races. As the study of the early child-hood of every man exposed one to the danger of striking against the original and undisguised meaning of these misinterpreted complexes, it was, therefore, thought best to make it a rule to tarry as little as possible at this past and to place the greatest emphasis on the return to the conflict. Here, moreover, the essential things are not at all the incidental and personal, but rather the general, that is to say, the "non-fulfilment of the life-task." Nevertheless, we know that the actual conflict of the neurotic becomes comprehensible and solvable only if it can be traced back into the patient's past history, only by following along the way that his libido took when his malady began.

How the New Zürich therapy has shaped itself under such tendencies I can convey by means of reports of a patient who was himself obliged to experience it.

"Not the slightest effort was made to consider the past or the transferences. Whenever I thought that the latter were touched, they were explained as a mere symbol of the libido. The moral instructions were very beautiful and I followed them faithfully, but I did not advance one step. This was more distressing to me than to the physician, but how could I help it?—Instead of freeing me analytically, each session made new and tremendous demands on me, on the fulfilment of which the overcoming of the neurosis was supposed to depend. Some of these demands were: inner coneen-tration by means of introversion, religious meditation, living together with my wife in loving devotion, etc. It was almost beyond my power, since it really amounted to a radical transformation of the whole spiritual man. I left the analysis as a poor sinner with the strongest feelings of contrition and the very best resolutions, but at the same time with the deepest discouragement. All that this physician recommended any pastor would have advised, but where was I to get the strength?"

It is true that the patient had also heard that an analysis of the past and of the transference should precede the process. He, how-ever, was told that he had enough of it. But as it had not helped

him, it seems to me that it is just to conclude that the patient had
not had enough of this first sort of analysis. Not in any case has
the superimposed treatment which no longer has the slightest claim
to call itself psychoanalysis, helped. It is a matter of wonder that
the men of Zürich had need to make the long detour via Vienna to
reach Bern, so close to them, where Dubois cures neuroses by ethical
encouragement in the most indulgent fashion.[19]

The utter disagreement of this new movement with psychoanalysis naturally shows itself also in its attitude towards repression,
which is hardly mentioned any more in the writings of Jung; in
the utter misconstruction of the dream which Adler, ignoring the
dream-psychology, confuses with the latent dream-thoughts, and
also in the lack of understanding of the unconscious. In fact this
disagreement can be seen in all the essential points of psychoanalysis.
When Jung tells us that the incest-complex is only "symbolic,"
that it has "no real existence," that the savage feels no desire
towards the old hag but prefers a young and pretty woman, then one
is tempted to assume in order to dispose of apparent contradiction
that "symbolic" and "no real existence" only signify what is
designated as "existing unconsciously."

If one maintains that the dream is something different from the
latent dream-thoughts, which it elaborates, one will not wonder that
the patients dream of those things with which their mind has been
filled during the treatment, whether it be the "life-task" or being
"above" or "below." Certainly the dreams of those analyzed are
guidable in a similar manner as dreams can be influenced by the
application of experimental stimuli. One may determine a part of
the material that occurs in the dream, but this changes nothing in
the nature and mechanism of the dream. Nor do I believe that the
so-called "biographical" dream occurs outside of the analysis. On

[19] I know the objections which stand in the way of using a patient's statements, and I, therefore, expressly state that my informant is as worthy of
credence as he is capable of judging this matter. He gave me this information without my request, and I make use of his communication without asking
his consent, because I cannot admit that any psychoanalytical technique should
lay claim to the protection of discretion.

the other hand, if we analyze dreams that occurred before the treatment began, or if attention is paid to what the dreamer adds to the stimuli supplied to him during the treatment, or if we avoid giving him any such task, then we can convince ourselves how far the dream is from offering tentative solutions of the life-task. For the dream is only another form of thinking; the understanding of this form can never be gained from the content of its thoughts, only the consideration of the dream-work will lead to it.

The effective refutation of Jung's misconceptions of psychoanalysis and his deviations from it is not difficult. Any analysis carried out in accordance with the rules, especially any analysis of a child, strengthens the convictions on which the theory of psychoanalysis rests, and repudiates the new interpretations of Adler's and Jung's systems. Jung himself, before he became enlightened, carried out such an analysis of a child and published it.[20] It remains to be seen if he will undertake a new interpretation of this case with the help of another "uniform new tendency of the facts," to give Adler's expression used in this connection.

The opinion that the sexual representation of "higher" ideas in the dream and in the neurosis is nothing but an archaic manner of expression, is naturally irreconcilable with the fact that these sexual complexes prove to be in the neurosis the carriers of those quantities of libido which have been withdrawn from the real life. If it were only a question of sexual jargon, nothing could thereby be altered in the economy of the libido itself. Jung himself admits this in his "Darstellung der psychoanalytischen Theorie," and formulates, as a therapeutic task, that the libido investing the complexes should be withdrawn from them. But this can never be accomplished by rejecting the complexes and forcing them towards sublimation, but only by the most exhaustive occupation with them, and by making them fully conscious. The first bit of reality with which the patient has to deal is his malady itself. Any effort to spare him this task points to an incapacity of the physician to help

[20] Experiences Concerning the Psychic Life of the Child, translated by A. A. Brill, American Journal of Psychology, April, 1910.

him in overcoming his resistances, or to a fear on the part of the physician as to the results of this work.

I would like to say in conclusion that Jung, by his "modifications" has furnished psychoanalysis with a counterpart to the famous knife of Lichtenberg. He has changed the hilt, has inserted into it a new blade, and because the same trademark is engraved on it he requires of us that we regard the instrument as the former one.

On the contrary, I believe I have shown that the new theory which desires to substitute psychoanalysis signifies an abandonment of analysis and a secession from it. Some may be inclined to fear that this defection may be more unfortunate for the fate of psychoanalysis than any other because it emanates from persons who once played so great a part in the psychoanalytic movement and did so much to further it. I do not share this apprehension.

Men are strong so long as they represent a strong idea. They become powerless when they oppose it. Psychoanalysis will be able to bear this loss and will gain new adherents for those lost.

I can only conclude with the wish that the fates may prepare an easy ascension for those who found their sojourn in the underworld of psychoanalysis uncomfortable. May it be vouchsafed to the others to bring to a happy conclusion their works in the deep.

www.ingramcontent.com/pod-product-compliance
Lightning Source LLC
Chambersburg PA
CBHW051504270326
41933CB00021BA/3468